Tough MACHINES

ACKNOWLEDGMENTS

The publishers would like to thank the following sources for the use of their photographs:

KEY A=Alamy B=Bridgeman CO=Corbis F=Fotolia FLPA=Frank Lane Picture Agency GI=Getty Images IS=istockphoto.com N=Newscom NPL=Nature Picture Library R=Reuters RF=Rex Features SPL=Science Photo Library S=Shutterstock SS=Superstock TF=Topfoto
t=top, a=above, b=bottom/below, c=center, l=left, r=right, f=far, m=main, bg=background

COVER Patrick Pleul/dpa/CO **BACK COVER** kaband/S **1** kaband/S **2** Pedro Nogueira/S **3**(bg) marino bocelli/S (strip, left to right) Kamira/S, Gyuszko-Photo/S, Christoffer Hansen Vika/S, Oleksiy Mark/S, Gentoo Multimedia Limited/S, **4–5** Patrick Pleul/dpa/CO, **6–7** stockshoppe/S, **6–7**(bg) Elenamiv/S, **6**(bl) Ivan Alvarado/R, **6**(cl) Marykit/S, **6**(cr) EtiAmmos/S, **6**(tr) ALMA (ESO/NAOJ/NRAO), **6**(tr) SVLuma/S, **7**(b) Mekl/S, **7**(b) U.S. Navy, **7**(t) Gleb Garanich/CO, **8–9**(bg) Angelo Giampiccolo/S, **8**(bl) Ashiga/S, **8**(br) Rechitan Sorin/S, **8**(c) Patrick Pleul/dpa/CO, **9**(br) Transtock/CO, **9**(cl) Marcus Lyon/GI, **9**(tr) antoni halim/S, **9**(tr) kaband/S, **10–11**(bg) Damen Dredging Equipment, **10**(bl) Stringer Sri Lanka/R, **10**(bl) Piyato/S, **10**(c) D, **11**(br) NASA/Science Faction/SS, **11**(tr) Sever180/S, **12–13**(b) Oleksandr Kalinichenko/S, **12–13**(c) David Gowans/A, **12**(b) Haakman, **12**(l) Kittisak/S, **12**(tl) Natykach Nataliia/S, **13**(tr) The Manitowoc Company, Inc., **14–15**(c) PRESNIAKOV OLEKSANDR/S, **14–15**(bg) Cristian Zamfir/S, **14–15**(bg) bluecrayola/S, **14**(bl) saasemen/S, **14**(bl) Gwoeii/S, **14**(br) caesart/S, **14**(c) Jarous/D, **14**(col) Robert Jakatics/S, **14**(cr) andras_ csontos/S, **14**(tl) ZargonDesign/IS, **15**(bl) Bill McCay/WireImage/GI, **15**(r) VolvoCE, **15**(tc) TFoxFoto/S, **16–17**(bg) Cardens Design/S, **16–17**(c) JACK FIELDS/SPL, **16**(br) Antje Fitzner/ NEEM, **16**(cl) Parys Ryszard/S, **17**(br) Sandvik, **17**(cr) Sandvik, **17**(tr) Rocket Design, **17**(tr) Anteromite/S, **18–19** Arnd Wiegmann/R, **18–19** STILLFX/S, **18**(b) Lyhne/MCT/N, **18**(bl) Eugene Chernetsov/S, **18**(tl) Roobcio/S, **18**(tl) isaravut/S, **19**(br) Jacek Filipiak/Sandvik, **19**(c) Construction Photography/CO, **19**(tr) qaphotos.com/A, **20–21** iadams/S, **20–21**(bg) Alexander Vasilyev/S, **20–21**(bg) alexkar08/S, **20**(br) Andrew Linnett/UK MOD, **20**(tr) Andrew Linnett/UK MOD, **21**(bl) Fotosearch/S, **21**(l) U.S. Navy/CO, **21**(tr) Solent News/RF, **22–23** Jack1e/S, **22–23**(bg) Emelyanov/S, **22**(bl) PinnacleAnimates/S, **22**(br) Darren Greenwood/Design Pics/CO, **22**(tl) Snowball/S, **23**(br) ALEXIS ROSENFELD/SPL, **23**(l) Oshkosh, **23**(t) Jeff Thrower/S, **23**(tr) Powell John/Glow Images, **23**(tr) mack2happy/S, **24–25** Dmitro2009/S, **24**(b) STEFAN THOMAS/epa/CO, **24**(c) NBC NewsWire/GI, **24**(tl) Serg Zastavkin/S, **25**(b) Stocktrek Images/GI, **25**(bl) Neirfy/S, **25**(c) Galen Rowell/CO, **25**(t) Matthias Scholz/A, **25**(t) T.W. van Urk/S, **26–27** Molodec/S, **26–27** Grei/S, **26–27**(bg) Africa Studio/S, **26**(b) Rolls-Royce plc, **26**(b) Viktorus/S, **26**(tl) ctrlaplus/S, **26**(tr) Teamdaddy/S, **27**(b) Pakhnyushcha/S, **27**(bc) NASA, **27**(br) NASA, **27**(br) vovan/S, **27**(c) RoyStudio.eu/S, **27**(c) Wartsilia, **27**(cl) Rolls-Royce plc, **27**(cr) Koenigseg, **27**(cr) Andrey_Kuzmin/S, **27**(tl) Maersk, **27**(tr) Borodaev/S, **27**(tr) Andrey Eremin/S, **28–29** Bork/S, **28–29** IgorGolovniov/S, **28–29** Kittisak/S, **28–29**(bg) Peter Ginter/Science Faction/SS, **28**(bl) donatas1205/S, **28**(cl) Monty Rakusen/GI, **28**(cl) marino bocell/S, **28**(tl) jordache/S, **29**(br) EdStock/IS, **29**(tr) MONTY RAKUSEN/SPL, **30**(bl) Dario Sabljak/S, **30**(bl) Zorandim/S, **30**(br) Igorsky/S, **30**(tl) I. Pilon/S, **30**(tl) haak78/S, **30**(tr) Gyuszko-Photo/S, **31**(b) dvande/S, **31**(bl) Prisma Bildagentur AG/A, **31**(t) pixelprof/IS, **31**(t) Gautier Willaume/S, **32**(bl) AFP/GI, **32**(l) Ints Vikmanis/S, **32**(r) J.D.S/S, **32**(tl) The Paper Street Design Company/S, **32**(tl) The Paper Street Design Company/S, **32**(tr) AFP/GI, **33**(br) Ho New/Reuters/CO, **33**(cl) NASA/CARNEGIE MELLON UNIVERSITY/SPL, **33**(r) NASA, **34–35** Matthias Pahl/S, **34–35**(bg) kanate/S, **34–35**(bg) Bobboz/S, **34**(bc) Mike Fisher KRT/N, **34**(cl) ESA, **34**(cr) NASA, **35**(br) ESA/C.Carreau/NASA, **35**(br) Andrey Zyk/S, **35**(c) NASA, **35**(tr) NASA, **36–37** Andrey Zyk/S, **36**(bl) Benjamin Haas/S, **36**(c) Konstanttin/S, **36**(cr) Virgin Oceanic/RF, **36**(l) dny3d/S, **36**(tc) argus/S, **36**(tc) ALEXIS ROSENFELD/SPL, **37**(c) Triton Submarines, **37**(cl) WHOI, **37**(cr) RF, **37**(r) argus/S, **38–39** Environment Agency, **38–39** cristapper/S, **38**(tl) siro/S, **39**(br) Julie Dermansky/Julie Dermansky/CO, **39**(cl) Royal BAM Group/Delta Marine Consultants, **39**(tc) PAUL WOOTTON/SPL, **39** S, **39** R-studio/S

All other photographs are from: Corel, digitalSTOCK, digitalvision, Dreamstime, Fotolia.com, iStockphoto.com, John Foxx, PhotoAlto, PhotoDisc, PhotoEssentials, PhotoPro, Stockbyte

Every effort has been made to acknowledge the source and copyright holder of each picture. The publishers apologise for any unintentional errors or omissions.

Tough MACHINES

Ian Graham
Consultant: Clint Twist

Miles Kelly

CONTENTS

Hauling Power	6
Earth Movers	8
Shaping the Seabed	10
Weight Lifters	12
Smash and Destroy	14
Drilling Force	16
Colossal Tunnelers	18
Armor Plate	20
Tough Rescuers	22
Subzero Heroes	24
Mighty Powerplants	26
Bash and Shape	28
Car Crushers	30
Rugged Robots	32
Far-out Explorers	34
Deepest Divers	36
Sea Defenders	38
Index	40

◀ A group of engineers are dwarfed by the gigantic bucket-wheel excavator that they are operating at an opencast mine.

HAULING Power

The toughest transport jobs are carried out by machines able to carry the biggest and heaviest loads. At sea, heavy-lift ships ferry colossal cargoes. On land, Herculean mining trucks haul heavy ore, while rugged transporters with dozens of wheels move awkward and outsize loads. In the air, gravity-defying cargo planes can transport enormous payloads weighing up to 550,000 lb (250 tons).

◄ An enormous ALMA transporter hauls a 253,000-lb (115-ton) radio telescope up a mountain in Chile's Atacama Desert.

A COLOSSAL 28-WHEELER
Two specially built transporters are being used to move 50 radio telescopes to a new space observatory on a high plateau in Chile. Named Otto and Lore, each 387,000-lb (130-ton) vehicle has 28 wheels to spread its heavy load and two mighty engines to power it the 17 mi (27 km) to the observatory.

Mining monsters
Vast quantities of ore are brought out of mines to be processed into metals. The biggest trucks in the world are used for this work. Fully loaded, they can weigh the same as 400 family cars. Each of their tires stands about 11 ft (3.5 m) tall and costs $42,500 (£27,500).

LAND

CATERPILLAR 797F
MAXIMUM LOAD:
800,000 LB (363 TONS)

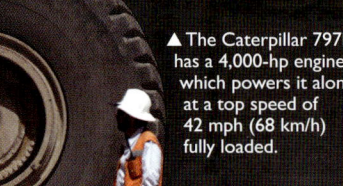

▲ The Caterpillar 797F has a 4,000-hp engine, which powers it along at a top speed of 42 mph (68 km/h) fully loaded.

Air cargo giant

When an extralarge or superheavy cargo needs to be carried by air, a unique cargo plane is pressed into service. There are freighter versions of airliners such as the Boeing 747, but for some cargoes there is just one machine for the job. The Antonov An-225 *Mriya* (Dream) was built in the 1980s to carry spaceplanes for the Soviet space program. It is still in service today as a heavy-lift cargo transporter.

THE ANTONOV An-225 CARGO PLANE HAS SET MORE THAN 200 AVIATION RECORDS.

▲ The Antonov An-225 can carry freight inside its cavernous cargo cabin or fixed to the top of its fuselage.

AIR

ANTONOV An-225
MAXIMUM LOAD:
550,000 LB (250 TONS)

Sea haulers

Semisubmersible heavy-lift ships carry oversized or heavy cargoes that other ships cannot. To load, the ship takes in seawater to make it sink until its deck is below water. The ship maneuvers underneath its cargo and then pumps out the water so that it rises again, with the cargo now on its deck.

▼ The MV *Blue Marlin*, a semisubmersible ship, transports a 380-ft- (116-m-) long floating radar station with ease.

SEA

MV BLUE MARLIN
MAXIMUM LOAD:
168 MILLION LB
(76,000 TONS)

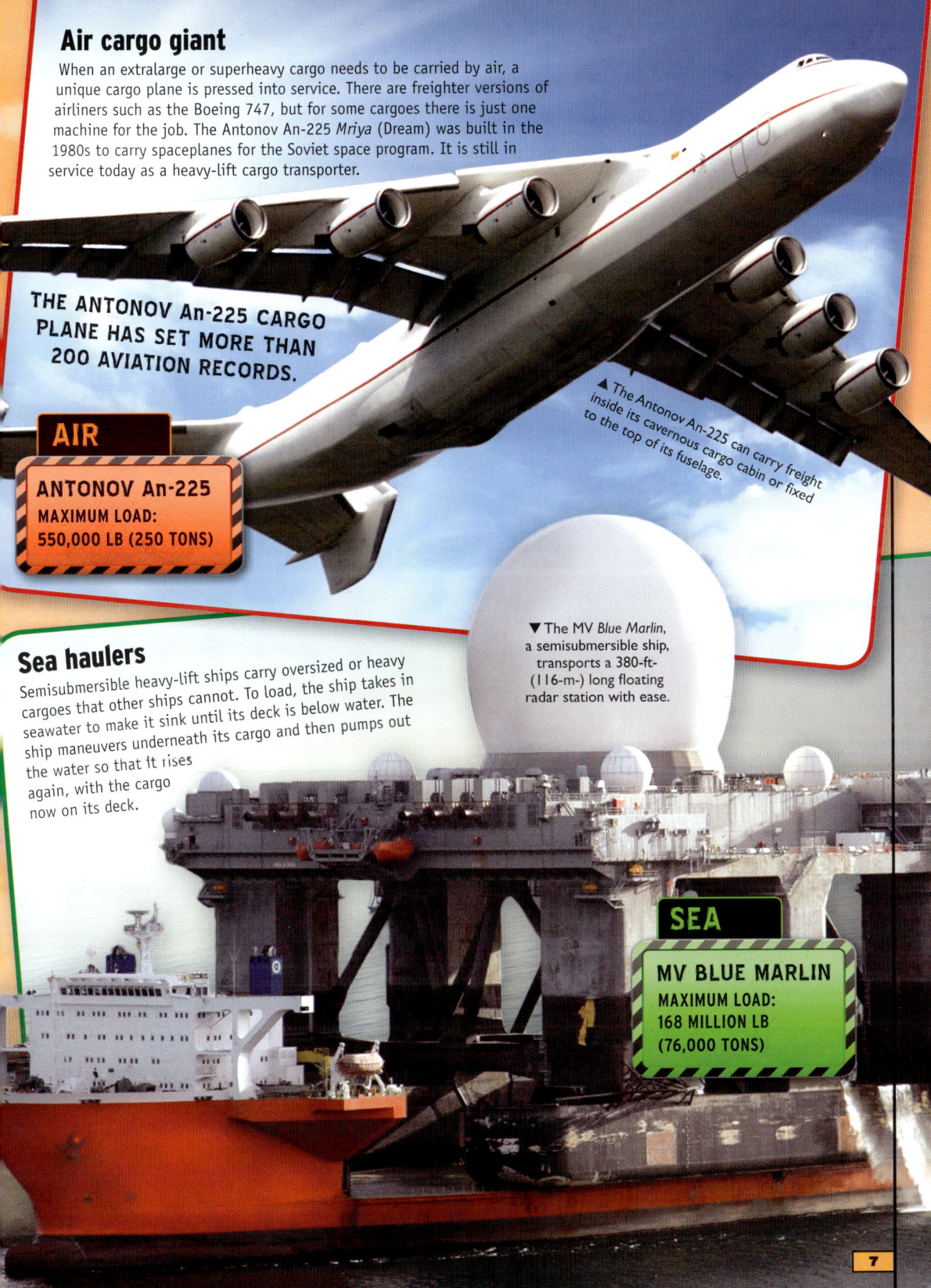

EARTH Movers

The biggest digging machines do one of the most formidable jobs there is. In mines and quarries, their enormous metal buckets tear into the ground, gouging out vast amounts of metal ore, coal, and earth. These giant diggers are aided by earth-moving machines such as bulldozers and loaders.

▶ In surface mines, bucket-wheel excavators strip away the earth and rock lying on top of coal. This one works in the Nochten open-pit mine in Germany.

Bucket beast

Giant bucket-wheel excavators are the biggest land machines ever made. They have a large rotating wheel attached to a long, counterweighted boom, which is pushed into the ground. As the wheel turns, buckets around its rim scoop up rock and earth. The biggest bucket-wheel excavator, Bagger 293, is 740 ft (225 m) long, 315 ft (96 m) tall, and its bucket wheel is more than 70 ft (21 m) across.

▶ Walking diggers are used to excavate on the roughest, steepest terrain, where most excavators cannot go.

WALKING DIGGERS

Excavators usually run on tracks to spread their weight over a bigger area and stop them from sinking into soft ground. The Menzi Muck A91 excavator is different—it can walk! The driver can move each of the wheels independently to make the excavator walk up steep slopes and over boulders. Spiked feet extend out from the wheel arms, into the ground, for better stability.

Mega loaders

Mining trucks have to be loaded quickly—they cost millions to buy and run, so time spent standing idle is expensive. Giant loaders are designed specially to fill these mega trucks. A large loader's bucket can scoop up tons of material, and raise it up more than 20 ft (6 m) in the air. This allows the loader to deposit the load in the center of the truck, keeping it balanced.

Oil-powered muscle

The most widely used digging machines are hydraulic excavators, but only the supersized variants of these work in the mining industry. Equipped with a cavernous bucket up to 18.5 ft (5.5 m) wide, attached to a mechanical arm, a hydraulic excavator digs, lifts, and loads rock and earth. The high-pressured oil in the hydraulic system is controlled by the driver, and generates energy to move the arm and bucket.

▲ A gigantic hydraulic power shovel can excavate almost 200,000 lb (90 tons) of rock with every scoop.

THE BIGGEST BUCKET-WHEEL EXCAVATOR CAN DIG ENOUGH EARTH IN A DAY TO FILL 96 OLYMPIC-SIZED SWIMMING POOLS.

▶ A huge engine provides the power a loader needs. The largest loaders have engines the size of a small family car.

Super dozers

Bulldozers are tough earth-moving machines. The biggest kind, Komatsu D575, is known as a super dozer. It has a 12-ft- (3.5-m-) long blade, which weighs around 22,400 lb (10 tons). Powered by a 1,150-hp engine, the dozer can push more than 330,000 lb (150 tons) of earth—the same weight as 30 elephants. If the ground is hard, a clawlike ripper at the rear of the dozer is lowered to break it up.

▲ This Komatsu D575 super dozer is as powerful as a supercar but about 90 times heavier.

9

SHAPING the Seabed

The shape of the seabed sometimes has to be altered, usually to deepen waterways for shipping. Ships called dredges, equipped with scoops, cutters, and suckers, carry out this underwater excavation. Dredges also mine sand and gravel from the seabed to supply the construction industry, or pump it onto the shore to restore eroded beaches and create new land.

◀ Bucket chain dredges are used for clearing shallow waterways. The biggest can scoop up 500,000 cu ft (14,150 cu m) of mud per hour.

Chain of buckets

The bucket dredge is a heavy-duty digging machine that can work from the shore or be mounted on a ship. The buckets are fixed to a continuous chain, like a huge bicycle chain, which is circulated by a motor. Beneath the water, the buckets scrape the seabed, scooping up mud, then empty the material into a chute as they are tipped upside down.

▶ A dredge sucks up and pumps out sand from the seabed. This is called "rainbowing."

Heavy metal spuds anchor the ship in position

▲ The biggest cutter suction dredges can reshape the seabed in water more than 100 ft (30 m) deep.

Spraying sand

A dredge can store the sand it excavates from the seabed in tanks inside the ship. When the tanks have to be emptied, the sand can be sent ashore through an underwater pipeline, but it's easier and less expensive to siphon it straight out of the ship. Powerful pumps on the ship can spray the sand onto a beach to build up the sand level, or to create a new artificial island.

A frame called a "ladder" supports the suction tube

Cutter suckers

For large-scale operations where the seafloor is hard, cutter suction dredges are used. This kind of ship is equipped with a rotating cutter head at the end of its suction tube. Before dredging, the ship drops metal poles called spuds into the seabed to anchor it. Then, as the ship moves from side to side, the cutter carves the rocky bed into small pieces, which are sucked up to the ship for disposal.

A clamshell dredge bucket is raised from the seabed full of silt.

ABOUT ONE FIFTH OF THE NETHERLANDS IS MADE OF EARTH DREDGED FROM THE SEABED.

Scooping mud

Grab dredges are used to excavate in shallow water. The grab, usually a two-piece, hinged bucket called a clamshell, is suspended on a wire from a crane that is fixed to a ship. It is lowered in the "open" position to the seabed, then closed to bite into the sediment.

The suction tube sucks up the loosened material

MAKING ISLANDS

A series of artificial islands have been built off the coast of Dubai by dredging. Ten of the world's biggest dredges vacuumed sand from the bottom of the Persian Gulf and piled it up to create the islands. Each ship filled its onboard tanks in less than an hour and then pumped the sand out fast enough to fill an Olympic-sized swimming pool in four minutes.

▶ The Palm Jumeirah island was created from 3.5 billion cu ft (100 million cu m) of rock and sand dredged from the bottom of the Persian Gulf.

The cutting head grinds up rock

11

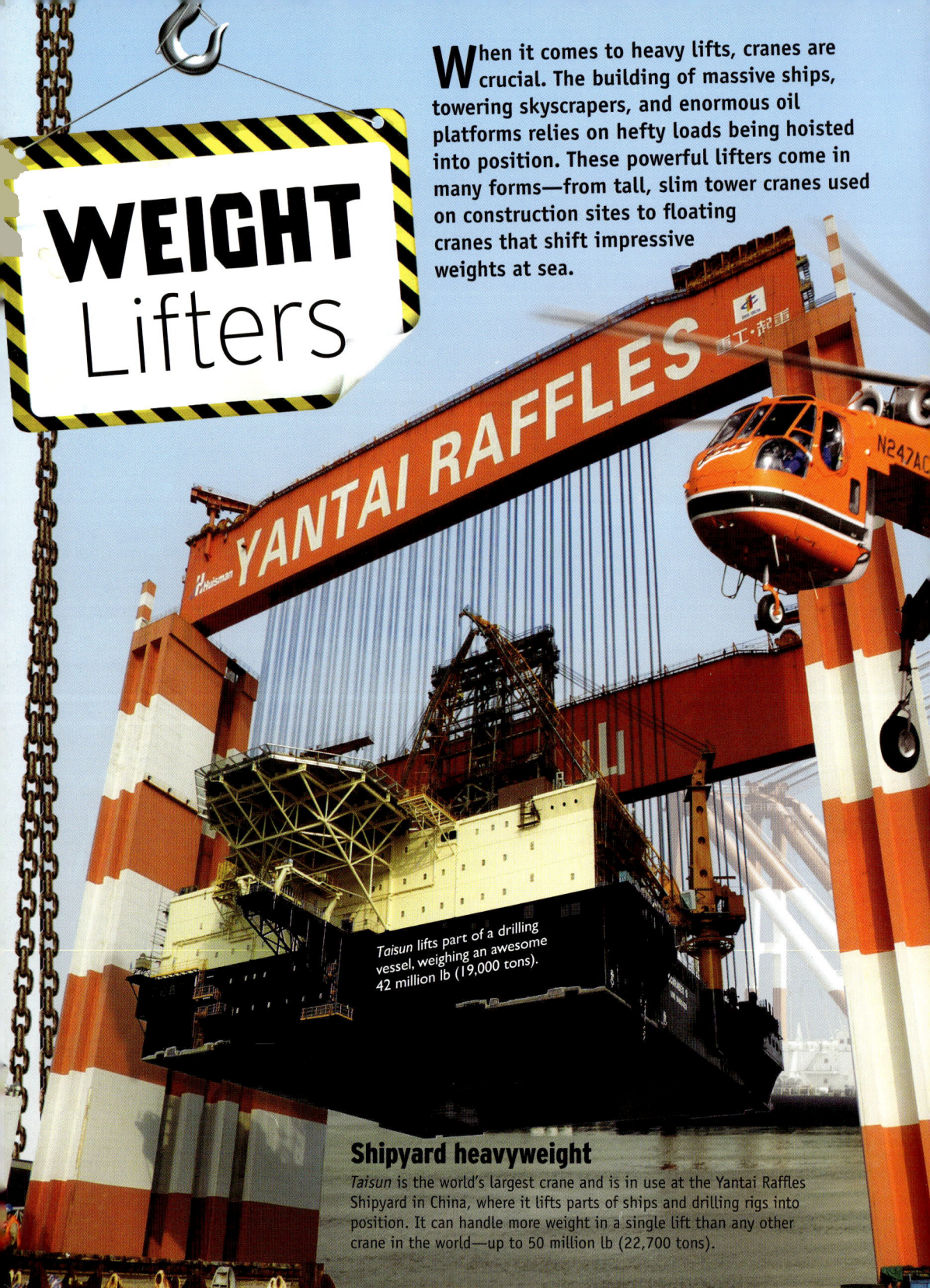

WEIGHT Lifters

When it comes to heavy lifts, cranes are crucial. The building of massive ships, towering skyscrapers, and enormous oil platforms relies on hefty loads being hoisted into position. These powerful lifters come in many forms—from tall, slim tower cranes used on construction sites to floating cranes that shift impressive weights at sea.

Taisun lifts part of a drilling vessel, weighing an awesome 42 million lb (19,000 tons).

Shipyard heavyweight

Taisun is the world's largest crane and is in use at the Yantai Raffles Shipyard in China, where it lifts parts of ships and drilling rigs into position. It can handle more weight in a single lift than any other crane in the world—up to 50 million lb (22,700 tons).

THE TOP SECTION OF THE CN TOWER IN TORONTO, CANADA, WAS LIFTED INTO POSITION BY AN S-64 AIRCRANE, NICKNAMED "OLGA."

Sky-high lifters

When construction jobs need just one or two heavy lifts, bespoke mobile or telescopic cranes are brought in to tackle the assignments. They are mounted on trucks or transported in pieces and built specially for each challenging task. Telescopic portable cranes are made of tubes that slide inside each other, making them easy to put up and take down.

The Grove GTK 1100 telescopic tower crane can lift a 213,000-lb (95-ton) load to a height of 380 ft (115 m)—taller than 15 houses.

◄ Floating cranes are also called sheerlegs. A large sheerleg can lift more than 9 million lb (4,000 tons) of bulky weight.

▲ The Erickson S-64 Aircrane can lift loads weighing up to 13 tons.

Flying crane

Specialized helicopters are used to lift large loads when cranes are unable to do the job; for example if the site is too remote or awkward to maneuver in. Aerial cranes are used to carry felled trees from forests, transport outsize sections of buildings, and install ski lifts and power lines. Some models are adapted for firefighting, with a large water tank and a filling hose, and can deliver 30,000 gal (113,500 l) of water per hour.

Floating muscle

Loads that have to be lifted in ports, rivers, and out at sea are handled by floating cranes. These highly specialized vessels are used in the offshore construction, oil, and bridge-building industries. Some of the biggest floating cranes are semisubmersible. Before a big lift, they take in seawater and sink lower to give themselves extra weight and stability.

SMASH and DESTROY

Big buildings are constructed to last, so demolishing them is a difficult task. Sometimes explosives are used to blow them up, but more often buildings have to be taken down piece by piece. Only machines that can punch through concrete, slice through steel, and endure falling rubble are tough enough for the job.

Demolition diggers

Excavators are designed for digging, but they can be used for destruction, too. Using its strong mechanical arm and bucket, an excavator can tear down walls and ceilings. The bucket can also be replaced with more specialized tools for hammering, cutting, and smashing its way through metal and concrete.

Pulverizer
Jaws with rows of metal teeth bite through concrete, reducing it to rubble.

Hammer
Smashes up large blocks on the ground for easy transportation.

Heavy-duty destroyers

Demolition is tough, hazardous work, so excavators intended for this task are modified to be extrastrong and supertough. The cab windows are covered with metal grilles to shield against falling rubble. Heavy-duty, double-thickness doors reduce side-impact damage. Underneath, thick metal plating protects the vehicle from being damaged by jagged metal and other sharp debris on the ground. The cab may also be sound-dampened to prevent the operator suffering hearing damage.

MORE THAN 200 BUILDINGS WERE DEMOLISHED TO CLEAR LAND FOR THE 2012 OLYMPIC GAMES IN LONDON.

High-reach arm
Fitted with any attachment, a high-reach excavator's extralong arm can dismantle a building's upper floors.

Grapple
Gripping jaws handle and sort loose material and irregular-shaped loads.

Bucket
Edged with teeth, the bucket can push or pull down walls and move loads of heavy rubble for disposal.

Reach for the sky

The high-reach excavator has an extralong boom arm, designed to reach the parts of buildings that standard excavators cannot. Their longer arms, which are usually about 100 ft (30 m) in length, can stretch to the upper floors of a building and take it to pieces. Much longer arms are also available—up to 300 ft (90 m) in length.

SWINGING WRECKER

First used in the 19th century, the brutal wrecking ball is the traditional demolition tool. A heavy steel sphere weighing up to 6 tons was suspended from a crane and dropped or swung against a building to smash down its walls. Although simple and effective, this method is imprecise, and the ball difficult to control. Today, safer and more efficient methods, such as controlled blasting charges, have taken over.

▶ A wrecking ball's weight and brute force smash a building to bits.

DRILLING Force

Oil and gas production, mining, and major construction projects all involve drilling deep holes in the ground. Huge, supertough drills grind through thousands of feet of rock to reach oil and gas, and in mines they bore holes for explosives that blast valuable ore out of the earth. At the poles, specialized drills extract deep ice cores that hold precious information about Earth's climate.

▼ The largest augers can drill holes up to 10 ft (3 m) in diameter and more than 160 ft (50 m) deep.

Piles of drilling

Before a building's foundations are laid, an auger may be needed to bore holes. This supersized tool has a helix-shaped screwing blade, which carries the drilled earth upward as it drives deeper into the ground. The auger leaves a neat, deep hole, which is filled with liquid concrete and a steel reinforcing cage. This process is repeated to form a set of strong underground legs called piles.

Priceless ice cores

Scientists use drills to obtain crucial information held in the deep Antarctic ice. An ice core drill is more than 30 ft (10 m) long. It has a hollow metal barrel attached to one end, which collects the ice sample, or core, as it bores down. Each time the drill is lowered, it can retrieve a core up to 20 ft (6 m) long. Many cores are extracted from the same hole, down to a depth of 10,000 ft (3,000 m) or more, and pieced together on the surface. The deepest ice can tell us about the environment and climate more than 100,000 years ago.

THE TOUGHEST OIL WELL DRILL BITS ARE ENCRUSTED WITH DIAMONDS, MAKING THEM 50 TIMES STRONGER THAN STEEL.

This hollow drill has an ice core inside it. The core will be pushed out and packed in plastic to keep it clean.

Wells of oil

Drilling through solid rock to reach oil and gas requires a tough drilling machine. The end that cuts through the rock is called the drill bit. There are different types of bit depending on the hardness of the rock that's being drilled through. The most common type is the rotary bit. As it rotates, hard teeth grind the rock away.

DRILLING AN OIL WELL

Whether on land or at sea, oil rigs use the same drilling technique. The drill pipe with a cutting bit on the end hangs from a tower called a derrick. A motor rotates the pipe and the cutting bit bores into the ground. As the drill goes deeper, more sections of pipe are added until the drill reaches the required depth. Offshore drilling rigs in shallow water stand on the seabed, but deep-water drilling rigs use floating platforms.

▶ Typically, oil wells are about 5,000 ft (1,500 m) deep. However, some rigs can drill down to a depth of 40,000 ft (12,200 m).

▼ The operator of this rock drilling jumbo steers two rock drills mounted on arms.

▼ A rotary drill is lowered into an oil well. The drill is tipped with grinding teeth.

Jumbo drillers

Machines called drilling jumbos are used underground to extend mines and tunnels. A drilling jumbo has up to three computer-controlled robot arms, which each hold a drilling head precisely in position to bore into the solid rock simultaneously. The tough drills tear through 3–6 ft (1–2 m) of rock per minute. The bored holes are then packed with explosives and blasted to extend the mine or tunnel.

17

COLOSSAL Tunnelers

Some of the world's longest road and rail tunnels are dug by massive machines called tunnel boring machines (TBMs). The biggest TBMs weigh several thousand tons and are as long as four soccer fields. They move along underground like huge mechanical earthworms, carving tunnels out of the rock.

Grinding rock

A TBM works by pushing a cutter head—a rotating cutting disk—against the rock in front of it. As the cutter head spins slowly, its teeth grind away the rock. Conveyors carry the rock, or spoil, back through the machine, to rail wagons that take it to the surface. The machine can cut through 6 ft (2 m) of rock an hour.

▶ A tunneler scrambles across excavated rock in front of a TBM cutter head under the Alps.

Concrete tunnel lining

Gripper shoes

Spoil conveyor belt
Carries waste material away

Cockpit
TBM is controlled from here

Cutter head
Up to 49 ft (15 m) in diameter

Hydraulic motors

▲ To advance, a TBM's gripper shoes lock into the rock walls and push the machine forward.

Strong-arm tactics

A tunnel needs a strong lining to stop the weight of the ground above it from caving in. The lining is usually made of huge, heavy concrete blocks. Each block, or segment, can weigh several tons. A TBM has a powerful mechanical arm to pick up each segment and lift it into position against the tunnel wall.

▼ A worker checks the fit of the concrete blocks lining the Channel Tunnel between England and France.

STAYING ON COURSE

Steering a tunnel boring machine is tricky when you're underground surrounded by rock. One guidance system uses a laser to keep the machine on course. A pencil-thin beam of light from the laser is aimed down the tunnel to a target on the machine. The machine is steered left, right, up, or down to keep the light in the middle of the target.

▼ A red laser beam shines down a tunnel to guide a TBM on exactly the right path.

▶ A roadheader's cutter is covered with dozens of tough teeth called picks.

Custom cutters

Tunnels that are too short or awkwardly shaped for a tunnel boring machine are made by using explosives or a machine called a roadheader. It has a mechanical arm with a drum on the end that is covered with metal teeth. As the drum spins, the operator steers the arm to carve out any shape of tunnel or cavern.

ARMOR PLATE

ARMORED BRIDGE LAUNCHER

ONLY $200,000

Military vehicles have to work in some of the most difficult and dangerous conditions imaginable, often while under attack. Many are armored with thick metal plates to protect the crews inside. As well as protection, this also adds weight—a heavily armored tank can weigh up to 70 tons.

Got a river to cross? You need a bridge launcher. The British Titan model is built on a Challenger 2 tank chassis, so you know it's up to the job. It's probably the fastest and best-protected bridge launcher in the world. Within two minutes, the bridge is unloaded and laid by powerful computer-controlled hydraulic rams, without the crew even having to leave the vehicle!

VITAL STATS
Name: Titan Armored Vehicle Bridge Launcher
Manufacturer: BAE Systems
Top speed: 37 mph (59 km/h)
Weight: 69 tons
Engine: 1,200-hp Perkins CV12 diesel
Armament: 7.62-mm machine gun and space to carry man-portable antitank weapons
Crew: 3

MIGHTY MASTIFF

Troops to transport? Convoys to protect? The Mastiff is the ideal set of wheels for the job.

This six-wheeled powerhouse, based on the U.S. Army's Cougar armored vehicle, has proved itself in service with the British Army. Its heavy armor and shock-mounted seats give great blast protection and a thermal imager lets you drive it at night without lights.

This example is nearly new with only one previous owner—the British Army.

ONLY $400,000

VITAL STATS
Name: Mastiff Protected Patrol Vehicle
Manufacturer: Force Protection Industries (modified for the British Army by NP Aerospace)
Top speed: 55 mph (88 km/h)
Weight: 30 tons
Engine: 330-hp Caterpillar C-7 diesel
Armament: 7.62-mm general purpose machine gun, 12.7-mm heavy machine gun, or 40-mm automatic grenade launcher
Crew: 2 plus 8 passengers

ONLY $4 MILLION

PHENOMENAL FIREPOWER

This is your chance to own the best.

The Abrams is the main battle tank operated by the U.S. Army and Marine Corps, and has unrivaled armor protection.

With all the firepower you'll ever need, the lethal 4.7-in (119-mm) main gun is guided by a laser rangefinder and computer-controlled targeting system. As well as ground targets, it can fire at low-flying aircraft. With excellent maneuverability and speed, it's the ultimate offroad vehicle.

VITAL STATS
Name: Abrams M1A2 SEP main battle tank
Manufacturer: General Dynamics
Top speed: 42 mph (68 km/h)
Weight: 69.5 tons
Engine: 1,500-hp turbine
Main armament: 4.7-in (119-mm) gun
Crew: 4 (commander, driver, gunner, and loader)

DIG THIS!
THE ALL-NEW ARMORED LIMO

Not all armored vehicles are in military service. Leading politicians and businessmen often travel in cars that have been fitted with armor plates and bulletproof glass. Cash is transported between banks and businesses in armored security vehicles, and most police forces have some armored cars in their fleet.

ARMORED AMPHIBIAN

ONLY $150,000

Assault Amphibious Vehicle for sale—great condition, low mileage, and one careful owner—the Marine Corps.

Travel on land or in water, and take up to 25 friends with you—there's plenty of room in the back. An aluminum hull makes it light and fast, but its armor is tough enough to withstand any amount of small arms fire.

VITAL STATS
Name: AAV7A1 Assault Amphibious Vehicle
Manufacturer: BAE Systems
Top speed: 45 mph (72 km/h) on land, 8 mph (13 km/h) in water
Weight: 32 tons
Engine: 400-hp Cummins VT400 diesel
Armament: Mk19 grenade launcher, M2HB machine gun
Crew: 3 plus 25 passengers or 10,000 lb (4.5 tons) of cargo

TOUGH RESCUERS

If you're trapped on a sinking boat or in a burning building, you need help—fast! Luckily, all sorts of emergency vehicles and rescuers are ready to come to your aid. Fire trucks are equipped to deal with many emergencies, not just fires. There are also highly specialized rescue vehicles for dealing with aircraft fires and submarines trapped underwater.

▼ A rescue helicopter carrying doctors lands on a mountaintop to help injured climbers.

1. Air-sea rescue

From a mountainside accident to someone in trouble at sea, versatile rescue helicopters deal with a range of search and rescue emergencies. They can maneuver with extreme precision, hover in position, fly through tight spaces, and land and take off again in seconds. If there isn't a safe place to land, a helicopter can winch people up, and rush them to hospital if necessary.

2. High-level firefighting

When firefighters tackle a blaze high above ground level, they bring in fire trucks with a hydraulically powered, extending ladder. Some of these ladders have a turntable base, so they can pivot in any direction, and built-in water pipes capable of delivering 1,000 gal (3,785 l) of water per minute to the top. Some turntable ladders have a "basket" at the top, big enough to hold up to three firefighters.

▼ This fire truck ladder has several sections that can extend to a height of more than 100 ft (30 m).

22

Fighting aircraft fires

Aircraft fires are challenging. Aircraft fires are challenging to tackle, and Aircraft Rescue and Firefighting (ARFF) emergencies are vital. These specialized vehicles must be able to reach any part of an airport quickly, and go off-road if necessary. An ARFF's foam jets can spray thousands of gallons of fire-suppressing foam per minute to extinguish burning jet fuel. For fires inside the cabin, an attachment called a "snozzle" pierces the plane's hull and sprays in foam or dry chemicals.

▶ An ARFF's jets are aimed using joysticks in the cab and can spray water and foam as far as 300 ft (90 m).

JAWS OF LIFE

In a serious road accident, drivers may become trapped in their crushed vehicles. Firefighters use a set of powerful, hydraulic tools, called "Jaws of Life," which cut through metal and force doors open. For maximum strength, tipped with heat-treated steel. A rescue can take place within 15 minutes. "Jaws of Life" can even be used to cut off a car's roof if the casualty needs to be lifted out.

▶ A firefighter slices open a crashed car with hydraulic shears.

Underwater emergency

In the event of an emergency on a submarine underwater, rescue divers attend the scene in a submersible rescue vehicle. Able to dive to a depth of 1,600 ft (500 m), these subs are specially designed to lock onto the submarine's escape hatch, which can then be opened to let the trapped sailors climb aboard. Unmanned submersibles can also be sent to cut through cables or nets entangling a vessel.

▶ This NATO Submarine Rescue Vehicle can operate at depths with a crushing pressure of 900 lb/sq in.

SUBZERO Heroes

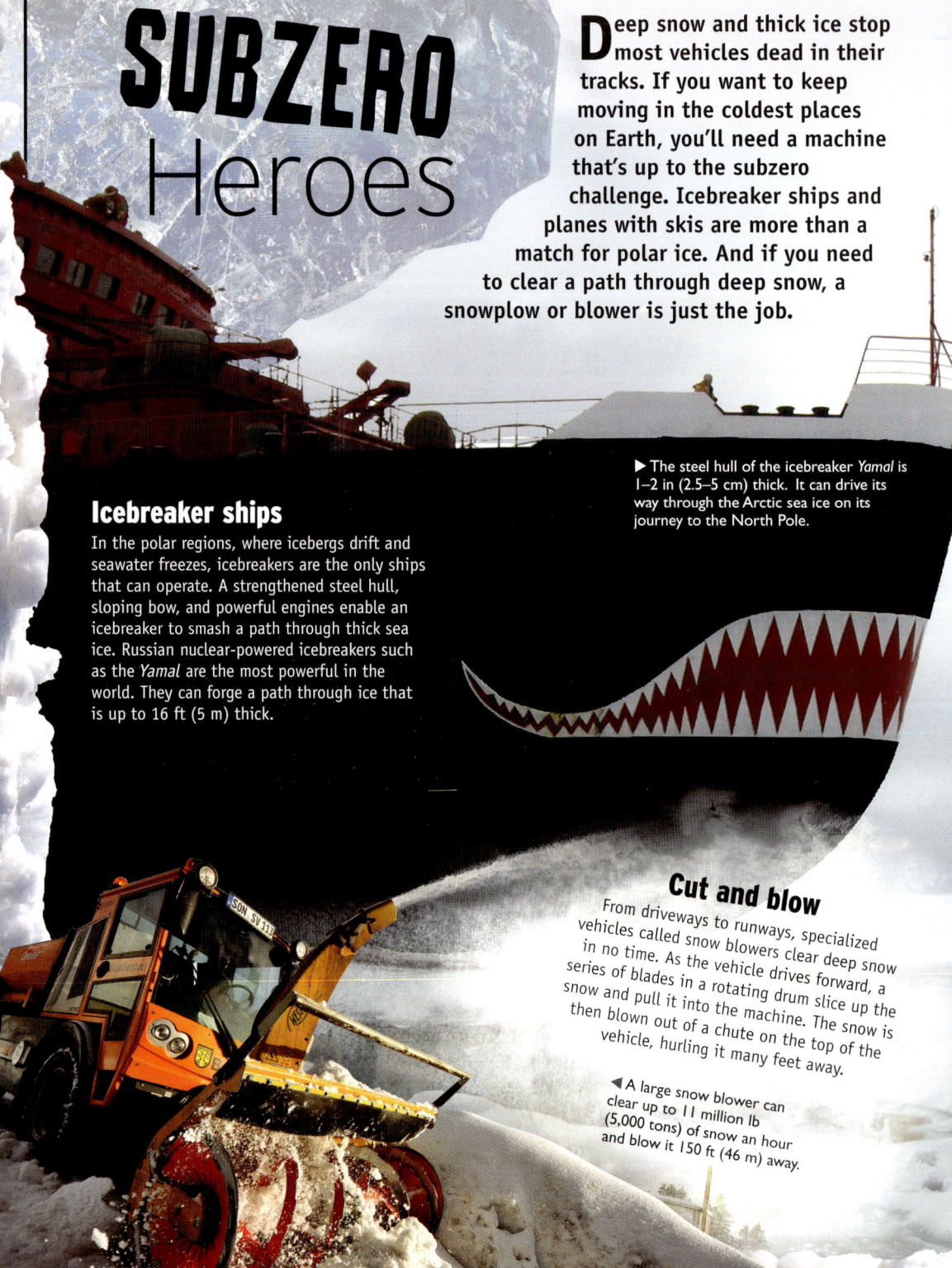

Deep snow and thick ice stop most vehicles dead in their tracks. If you want to keep moving in the coldest places on Earth, you'll need a machine that's up to the subzero challenge. Icebreaker ships and planes with skis are more than a match for polar ice. And if you need to clear a path through deep snow, a snowplow or blower is just the job.

▶ The steel hull of the icebreaker *Yamal* is 1–2 in (2.5–5 cm) thick. It can drive its way through the Arctic sea ice on its journey to the North Pole.

Icebreaker ships

In the polar regions, where icebergs drift and seawater freezes, icebreakers are the only ships that can operate. A strengthened steel hull, sloping bow, and powerful engines enable an icebreaker to smash a path through thick sea ice. Russian nuclear-powered icebreakers such as the *Yamal* are the most powerful in the world. They can forge a path through ice that is up to 16 ft (5 m) thick.

Cut and blow

From driveways to runways, specialized vehicles called snow blowers clear deep snow in no time. As the vehicle drives forward, a series of blades in a rotating drum slice up the snow and pull it into the machine. The snow is then blown out of a chute on the top of the vehicle, hurling it many feet away.

◀ A large snow blower can clear up to 11 million lb (5,000 tons) of snow an hour and blow it 150 ft (46 m) away.

Snow on the rails

When snow piles up on railroad tracks, snowplows are the machines to clear it. The simplest railroad snowplow has a wedge-shaped front, which forces the snow aside as the train speeds along. For the deepest snow, a rotary snowplow with spinning blades is used. The blades cut through deep, hard-packed snowdrifts, removing them from the tracks.

◀ A rotary snowplow's blades spin more than 100 times per minute, shredding the hardest snow to powder.

▶ The Sno-Cat has been used by scientists and explorers in the Arctic and Antarctic since 1951, and is still in use today.

Making tracks

Normal cars and trucks would get stuck in the deep snow of the polar regions, so tracked vehicles are the transport of choice for this frozen wilderness. Their wide, ribbed tracks not only spread their weight, stopping them from sinking in soft snow, but they also provide grip. As well as carrying personnel, these vehicles can tow sleds laden with up to 8 tons of equipment.

▼ A ski-equipped LC-130 takes off from an ice runway in Antarctica. Its two main skis are 20 ft (6 m) long and 5.5 ft (1.7 m) wide.

AN LC-130 HERCULES SKI PLANE CAN CARRY MORE THAN 26,000 LB (12 TONS) OF CARGO TO POLAR BASES.

Polar plane

At the poles, where snow and ice cover every solid surface, an airplane is the last vehicle you may expect to see. However, the LC-130 Hercules is a regular visitor. A fleet of LC-130s ferry scientists and equipment between research stations and camps in Antarctica. Their ski-equipped landing gear means that they can land on snow and ice.

MIGHTY POWERPLANTS

Beneath the hood, under the wing, and below deck, some of the most powerful engines can be found. Jet engines propel airliners through the atmosphere at just below the speed of sound and rockets thrust space vehicles into orbit. Back on Earth, piston engines boost supercars to incredible speeds and power colossal ships across the oceans.

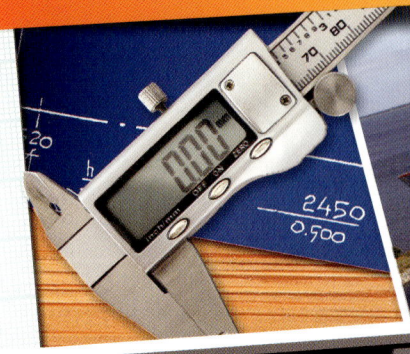

Superhot jets

The most advanced airliner engines, such as the Rolls-Royce Trent XWB, are remarkable machines. They power heavy aircraft laden with hundreds of passengers, thousands of miles around the world. They generate enormous thrust simply by compressing air, then heating it to make it expand. In fact, the air becomes so hot that it could melt the engine! These engines have to be designed carefully to withstand the incredible pressures generated inside the engine, and with clever cooling technology to stop overheating.

BYPASS AIR
90 percent of air sucked in by the fan bypasses the combustor, flows around it, and goes out the back of the engine. This produces most of the thrust.

	1 FAN	2 COMPRESSOR	3 COMBUSTOR
Pressure:	15 lb/sq in	120 lb/sq in	500 lb/sq in
Temperature:	176°F (80°C)	554°F (290°C)	2,700°F (1,480°C)

1 FAN
The fan sucks large quantities of air into the engine. Its blades are made of titanium.

FAN CASING
The casing surrounding the fan stops broken fan blades from flying out of the engine.

2 COMPRESSOR
The compressor is made up of many rotating, bladed fans. It squashes air to one fiftieth of its original volume.

3 COMBUSTOR
Inside this heat-resistant chamber, fuel is mixed with the air and ignited, creating high-energy expanding gases

Emma Maersk

MARINE MAMMOTH
The biggest cargo ships are powered by diesel engines the size of a house. The Emma Maersk is one of the biggest containerships ever built. To propel it across the ocean, it needs a massively powerful engine—the Wärtsilä RT-flex96C. This huge powerplant is 90 ft (27 m) long, 44 ft (13.5 m) high, and weighs a staggering 5.1 million lb (2,300 tons).

The RT-flex96C engine is the world's biggest diesel engine and powers the 1,300-ft- (400-m-) long containership, the Emma Maersk.

Koenigsegg Agera R

SWEDISH SUPERCAR
The most powerful street-legal cars pack ten times the power of a small family car. One such supercar, the Swedish-made Koenigsegg Agera R, has a 1,140-hp engine hidden under its sleek, streamlined body. This superpowerful engine and the car's carefully designed shape give the Agera R a 0–60 mph (0–97 km/h) time of 2.9 seconds and a top speed of 273 mph (440 km/h).

Airbus A350

4 TURBINE
The turbine spins at 10,000 rpm, powered by the jet of hot air leaving the engine.

4 TURBINE
500–900 lb/sq in
2,000–2,700°F (1,090–1,480°C)

HOT AIR
The air expands as it heats up and rushes out of the engine.

The Airbus A350 is powered by two Rolls-Royce Trent XWB engines. Each engine has 18,000 parts that have to work together seamlessly.

Saturn V

FABULOUS F-1
The Saturn V rocket that launched astronauts to the Moon weighed more than 6 million lb (2,700 tons). The most powerful rocket engines ever built got it off the ground—Rocketdyne F-1s. Each F-1 was 19 ft (5.8 m) long and weighed more than 9 tons. They had to withstand kerosene burning inside them at a temperature of 5,970°F (3,300°C).

Each F-1 rocket engine burns 670 gal (2,540 l) of kerosene and liquid oxygen every second.

BASH and Shape

Machines that make and shape metal generate searing temperatures and unimaginable forces. First, ore is heated in enormous glowing furnaces to extract the valuable metal. Then gigantic hammers, rollers, and lathes bash and shape the metal. These machines consume enormous amounts of energy—one large steel furnace uses as much electricity as 150,000 homes.

▼ Vertical lathes make parts with large diameters, such as giant wheel-shaped components for engines and turbines.

◄ Showers of sparks fly as a blast furnace pours out molten iron.

Metal turning

Jumbo versions of metal-shaping tools called lathes are used to manufacture circular parts such as wheels, axles, and shafts. The biggest lathes can handle huge workpieces weighing up to one million lb (450 tons). The lathe rotates the workpiece, and a cutting tool—made of a supertough material such as tungsten carbide—presses against it. With extreme precision, metal is gradually shaved off until the workpiece reaches the required shape.

Liquid steel

Steel is made in vast furnaces that work at extremely high temperatures. They heat tons of iron and recycled steel to about 3,000°F (1,650°C) to turn them into glowing liquid metal. A blast furnace blows oxygen through the mixture, providing extra energy to speed up the steel-making process. Then the molten steel is poured into giant buckets called ladles, which are carried away by crane to pour the steel into molds.

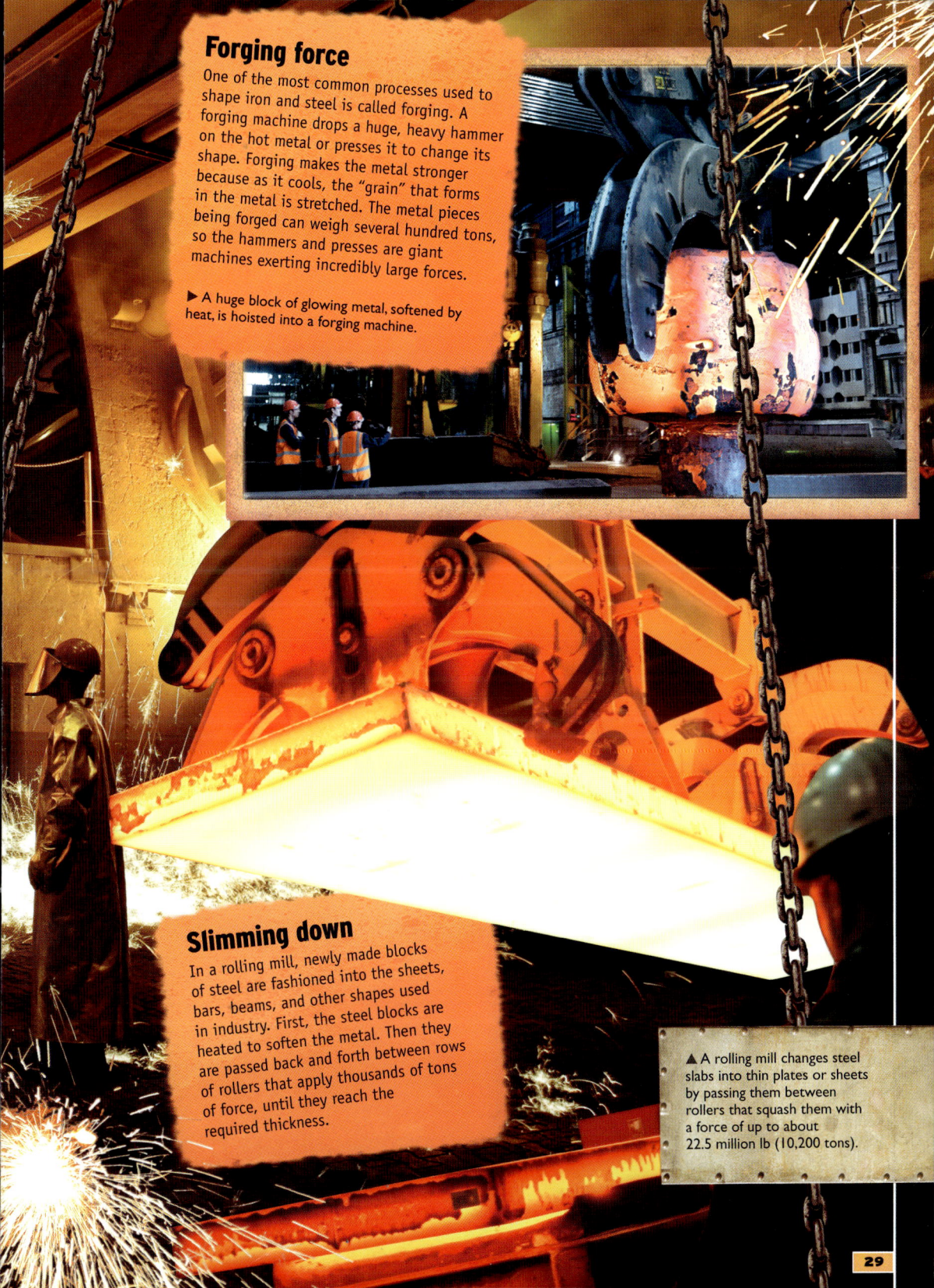

Forging force

One of the most common processes used to shape iron and steel is called forging. A forging machine drops a huge, heavy hammer on the hot metal or presses it to change its shape. Forging makes the metal stronger because as it cools, the "grain" that forms in the metal is stretched. The metal pieces being forged can weigh several hundred tons, so the hammers and presses are giant machines exerting incredibly large forces.

▶ A huge block of glowing metal, softened by heat, is hoisted into a forging machine.

Slimming down

In a rolling mill, newly made blocks of steel are fashioned into the sheets, bars, beams, and other shapes used in industry. First, the steel blocks are heated to soften the metal. Then they are passed back and forth between rows of rollers that apply thousands of tons of force, until they reach the required thickness.

▲ A rolling mill changes steel slabs into thin plates or sheets by passing them between rollers that squash them with a force of up to about 22.5 million lb (10,200 tons).

CAR CRUSHERS

Every year, millions of cars reach the end of their useful life, and a lineup of specialized metal-crunching machines help to dispose of them. First, vehicles are dismantled to recover and recycle useful parts and metals. Then machines crush them down, chew them up, and spit them out as scrap metal.

▲ A scrapyard grab punches through a car's body and picks it up as if it were a toy.

Step 1: GRIP!

Scrapped cars are picked up, moved around the scrapyard, and loaded into crushing and shredding machines by huge hydraulic grippers called grabs. The grab opens and closes like an outsize steel hand, and is able to lift up to 9 tons of weight. A grab can be fitted to the arm of a crane, or to an excavator's boom instead of a digging bucket.

THE LARGEST SHREDDER IN THE WORLD—THE LYNXS AT THE SIMS PLANT, SOUTH WALES—CAN SHRED 450 CARS PER HOUR.

RECYCLING SAVINGS

The recycling of vehicles is a multibillion dollar industry, because it recovers valuable materials such as metals. Recycled steel and iron don't need to be made from new. Every car recycled saves one ton of metal-containing rock called ore, and 1,400 lb (635 kg) of coal needed to process the ore.

An average car contains more than:
- 2,000 lb (907 kg) of steel
- 240 lb (110 kg) of aluminum
- 110 lb (50 kg) of rubber
- 50 lb (23 kg) of carbon
- 42 lb (19 kg) of copper
- 41 lb (18 kg) of silicon
- 22 lb (10 kg) of zinc

▼ A hydraulic crushing plate bears down with enormous force, pressing a car to less than half its original size.

Step 2: CRUSH!

When fuel, oil, batteries, glass, and other useful parts have been removed from scrapped cars, the car bodies are crushed in a hydraulic press. These powerful machines can exert crushing forces of up to 336,000 lb (150 tons) to squash car bodies flat. Another type of crusher compresses them into refrigerator-sized blocks called bales. This makes the cars easier to store and transport by truck to a recycling plant.

◀ Large car recycling plants can process up to 110 million lb (50,000 tons) of material per month.

▼ Rotors in the shredder spin at 175 mph (280 km/h), tearing cars to pieces.

Step 3: SHRED!

The compacted car bodies are fed into the "mouth" of a shredding machine. A series of heavy hammers on spinning rotors tear the car bodies into pieces smaller than a fist, which are carried along a conveyor belt to be sorted. Magnets separate the iron and steel from other metals and fans blow light plastic and cloth away. Finally, devices called eddy current separators sort the remaining metals from nonmetals by using electric currents.

RUGGED Robots

When a job is too dangerous for people, specially designed robots are readied for the task. They can search for survivors in unsafe disaster areas, investigate locations with lethal radiation levels, and operate in the airless void of space. When it comes to bomb disposal, the Police and Armed Forces' robot workforce carry out these high-risk missions.

TEODor
Job: Bomb disposal
Made by: Telerob, Germany
Special feature: Can be fitted with up to six cameras and armed with weapons and tools to deal with unexploded bombs

Robot rescuer

T-52 Enryu was designed to aid rescue in earthquake-hit zones. The robot stands 11 ft (3 m) tall and is strong enough to lift a car. It has two eight-jointed arms with claw attachments, which can lift debris to clear a path for a rescue team to reach possible survivors. Enryu is controlled by an operator in a cockpit inside the robot or, if this is too dangerous, using a control box from a safe distance.

T-52 ENRYU
Job: Aids rescue in disaster areas
Made by: Tmsuk, Japan
Special skill: Its two 20-ft- (6-m-) long arms can lift a combined weight of one ton

Intrepid assistant

TEODor is a small, tracked vehicle used by law enforcement agencies worldwide to dispose of explosives. Its tracks enable it to travel on rough terrain, and it is small enough to maneuver inside a house. TEODor is equipped with cameras, a movable arm, and specialized tools to investigate and disarm an explosive device. The robot is remotely controlled by an operator a safe distance away, who sees the robot's view through its cameras.

Volcano explorer

Active volcano craters may be searingly hot and full of toxic gases, but volcanologists prize samples collected from them to study past eruptions and predict future activity. In 1993, a walking robot called *Dante II* was developed to gather these samples. It had eight legs and, attached to an anchor cable, could rappel down sheer, uneven crater walls. When the target was reached, *Dante II* took samples and recorded measurements with its onboard instruments, and relayed data to controllers via satellite.

DANTE II
Job: Explore active volcano craters
Made by: Carnegie Mellon University, U.S.
Special skill: Can rappel down crater walls and walk over objects up to 3 ft (one meter) high

Space station robot

Since 2008, the International Space Station (ISS) has had a two-armed robot called the Special Purpose Dexterous Manipulator, or Dextre, on board. It's a "handyman" that works in the deadly conditions outside the ISS, especially in the great extremes of temperature—boiling hot in sunshine and freezing cold in shadow.

DEXTRE
Job: Maintenance of the ISS
Made by: MacDonald, Dettwiler, and Associates, Canada
Special feature: Two 11-ft- (3-m-) long robotic arms, equipped with tools

Robot investigator

Packbots are small enough to fit in a backpack and able to deal with a range of risky tasks. These robots are designed to withstand rough treatment—a Packbot can survive a 6-ft (1.8-m) drop onto concrete without damage. Treaded tracks help it climb over obstacles and can flip it upright if it is overturned. Following the 2011 Japanese tsunami, two Packbots were sent into Fukushima nuclear power plant to inspect its damaged reactors. The robots worked in high levels of radiation and sent back live video and temperature recordings.

PACKBOT
Job: Investigation and bomb disposal in dangerous locations
Made by: iRobot, U.S.
Special skills: Small, tough, and adaptable

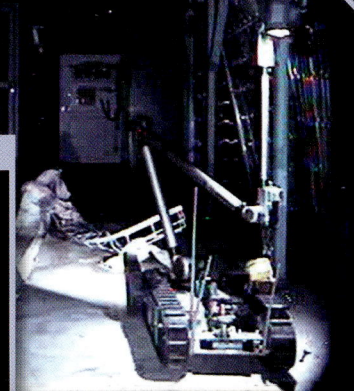

FAR-OUT Explorers

Space is a hostile environment. Spacecraft have to be able to survive conditions that would freeze or fry most machines on Earth. They must also keep working for many years—*Voyager 1* has been sending back data from its journey to the edge of the Solar System for more than 35 years.

A curious craft

The *Curiosity* rover landed on Mars in August 2012 to investigate if the planet once supported tiny life-forms. Temperatures on Mars are cold, so a heating system warms the rover, keeping its instruments operational. Six 20-in- (50-cm-) diameter wheels allow *Curiosity* to traverse rough terrain. It can collect samples for testing by scooping up soil or using its robotic arm to grind into rocks.

▼ The *Curiosity* rover is a nuclear-powered electric vehicle the size of a small car.

▲ The SOHO spacecraft generates electricity for its instruments from sunlight using its 31-ft- (9.5-m-) long solar panel array.

Studying the Sun

Storms on the Sun can affect us on Earth, so scientists are keen to study our nearest star. The Solar and Heliospheric Observatory (SOHO) spacecraft has been observing the Sun since 1996. It orbits a point in space about 930,000 mi (1.5 million km) away from Earth, where its instruments have an uninterrupted view of the Sun.

MERCURY

VENUS

EARTH

MARS

Planetary messenger

Mercury, the closest planet to the Sun, is being studied by the spacecraft *Messenger*. *Messenger* has to cope with temperatures as high as 700°F (370°C) and its instruments and electronics are kept at room temperature by a sunshade made of heat-resistant ceramic cloth. This also protects the craft from solar radiation.

◀ *Messenger* was launched in 2004 and went into orbit around the planet in 2011.

Frozen spacefarer

In 2006, a spacecraft called *New Horizons* was launched on a mission to the distant dwarf planet, Pluto. It is set to arrive in 2015. To cope with the intense cold at Pluto, *New Horizons* is covered with multiple layers of insulation. This is so effective at conserving heat that the craft had to cool itself while traveling through the inner Solar System to prevent it overheating.

▶ *New Horizons* has to withstand temperatures as low as -390°F (-234°C) at the edge of the Solar System.

PLUTO

NEPTUNE

URANUS

SATURN

JUPITER

Titan (moon)

Titan lander

As the *Cassini* spacecraft hurtled toward the ringed planet Saturn in 2004, it released a mini probe called *Huygens*, headed for Saturn's biggest moon, Titan. Very little was known about Titan, so *Huygens* had to be able to land on any surface, solid or liquid. It descended through Titan's thick atmosphere before bouncing and skidding to a stop, taking photographs on the way down and for 90 minutes after landing.

SPACECRAFT THAT EXPLORE THE OUTER PLANETS ARE POWERED BY NUCLEAR ENERGY, BECAUSE THEY TRAVEL TOO FAR FROM THE SUN TO USE SOLAR POWER.

1 Heat shield is released and instruments are activated before touchdown

2 Parachute slows descent

3 *Huygens* lands on surface of Titan at a speed of 16 ft/sec (5 m/sec)

▶ The *Huygens* probe descended through Titan's cloudy atmosphere by parachute.

35

DEEPEST DIVERS

Some of the most extreme conditions on Earth are found at the bottom of the ocean. The deepest parts of the ocean floor are 7 mi (11 km) below the surface and the pressure exceeds 16,000 lb/sq in. It is also freezing cold—just over 32°F (0°C)—and totally dark. Only the toughest submersibles can operate here.

DIVING ARMOR

Divers can descend to depths of more than 2,000 ft (610 m) wearing an Atmospheric Diving Suit (ADS). It is a jointed suit of armor, reinforced to withstand crushing water pressure 60 times higher than at the surface. Inside the suit, the pressure is the same as on the surface, so the diver can breathe normally with no risk of decompression sickness, known as "the bends."

Underwater flier

DeepFlight Challenger "flies" through the water like a plane, using upside-down wings to descend at a speed of 350 ft (110 m) per minute. To withstand the pressure at the deepest part of the ocean its slender hull is made of supertough carbon fiber and the viewing dome is made of quartz. Despite *DeepFlight Challenger* being relatively light at 3.5 tons, it is able to dive to the seafloor and return to the surface in only five hours.

▶ This French Navy rescue diver is wearing an ADS called a Newtsuit. A thruster backpack can propel the diver through the water.

BELOW 3,300 FT (1,000 M), THE OCEAN IS PITCH BLACK.

▶ Aquanauts including Sir Richard Branson plan to dive to the deepest parts of the world's five oceans in a *DeepFlight Challenger* submersible.

Robot sub

In 2009, *Nereus* became the third vehicle ever to explore Challenger Deep—the deepest point in the ocean. The unmanned submersible is made of light, ceramic material, which can endure huge pressures. It descended all the way to the seafloor trailing a hair-thin optical fiber, up to 25 mi (40 km) long, which was attached to a ship on the surface. This allowed *Nereus* to send back live video and images to the surface.

▶ The 3-ton submersible, *Nereus*, is powered by onboard battery packs, which enable it to stay submerged for up to 24 hours.

In design

The *36000* looks like an alien spaceship, but it's a submersible being built by Triton Submarines to take people to the deepest parts of the ocean. Its occupants—up to three people—will sit inside a thick glass dome, which becomes stronger the more pressure it is put under. It will be used by scientists for deep-ocean research and tourists who want to visit the deep-sea world.

▼ Triton's *36000* descends at 500 ft (150 m) per minute, reaching the deepest part of the ocean within about 75 minutes.

CHALLENGER DEEP—36,069 FT (10,994 M) BELOW SEA LEVEL—IS THE DEEPEST PLACE ON EARTH.

Deep-sea challenge

Movie director James Cameron is the third person to visit Challenger Deep, located at the bottom of the Mariana Trench in the Pacific Ocean, 36,069 ft (10,994 m) down. He made the journey in a submersible called *Deepsea Challenger*. Cameron sat inside a 2.5-in- (7.3-cm-) thick spherical steel chamber, housed in the 24-ft- (7-m-) tall craft, and looked out through a tiny viewport.

▶ *Deepsea Challenger* reached the deepest part of the ocean on March 26, 2012. Its 43-in (110-cm) crew sphere is big enough for just one person.

37

Sea Defenders

The forces of nature are formidable. Storm surges and exceptionally high tides can overwhelm coastal cities, and rising sea levels are making this problem worse. Mammoth mechanical barriers protect some of the world's biggest ports from flooding.

THE THAMES BARRIER

The U.K.'s capital city, London, is protected from flooding by a barrier across the River Thames, which flows through the city. The Thames Barrier's ten steel gates span 1,706 ft (520 m) from bank to bank. The four biggest gates in the middle weigh 7 million lb (3,200 tons) each.

Pier roof
Made of timber covered with stainless steel sheets to protect machinery inside

Rocking arm
Moved by two hydraulic cylinders in the pier roof to rotate the gate

▶ The barrier can protect London from a surge up to 7 ft (2 m) high, and to date the barrier has never been breached.

Central pier
Each central concrete pier is 36 ft (11 m) wide, 210 ft (65 m) long, and penetrates 50 ft (15 m) into the riverbed

Rising sector gate
Made of 2-in- (5-cm-) thick high-strength steel, designed to allow water and air in and out

PROTECTING LONDON

When "open," the Thames Barrier's gates lie flat on the riverbed in a curved trough. When forecasters predict the threat of flood, boat traffic on the river is ordered to stop and the machinery on the piers starts up. The hydraulic rocking arms rotate the gates, which rise up from the riverbed until they stand vertical. This forms an impassable barrier, keeping the surge of seawater out of London. When the threat passes, the machinery rotates the gates back and they disappear below the waves.

Gate rotates 90 degrees to stand upright and hold back a storm surge.

Tunnels
A pair of tunnels run beneath the Thames, providing access and services

Filter layer
A layer of stone blocks stops the riverbed from being washed away

Gravel layer
A deep layer of gravel laid over solid chalk bed

Sinking city

The Italian city of Venice is world-famous for its canals. It also suffers from frequent flooding. To make matters worse, Venice is slowly sinking into the mud it is built on. Engineers are laying 78 gates on the bed of the lagoon that surrounds the city. When the gates are closed, the lagoon will be sealed off from the sea. The project is called M.O.S.E. (Modulo Sperimentale Elettromeccanico), and is due to be completed in 2014.

◀ The gates that protect Venice are closed by pumping air into them. This makes them buoyant, so they stand upright.

▼ Each of the gates of Rotterdam's Maeslant barrier is 787 ft (240 m) long and 72 ft (22 m) high.

Floating giants

Rotterdam in the Netherlands is one of the world's busiest ports. If high sea levels pose a threat, the two huge steel gates of the Maeslant barrier—each the weight of two Eiffel Towers—seal the city off from the North Sea. Open, the gates sit in dry docks in the waterway walls. When needed, they are floated out until they meet. Then they are flooded with water to weigh them down.

▶ Gates in the New Orleans flood barrier stay open to let boats through unless a storm threatens the city.

SOUTHERN BRITAIN IS SLOWLY SINKING, INCREASING THE FLOODING RISK IN LONDON.

Storm barriers for New Orleans

In 2005, New Orleans, U.S., was devastated by a flood caused by Hurricane Katrina. Since then, the city's flood defenses have been rebuilt and improved. New Orleans is now protected by the world's largest storm surge barrier—a wall 2 mi (3.2 km) long and 32 ft (10 m) high, fortified with 350 mi (560 km) of embankments called levees. Rainfall and floodwater can also be pumped out of the city by the world's most powerful pumping station.

INDEX

Entries in **bold** refer to main subject entries; entries in *italics* refer to illustrations.

Abrams M1A2 SEP battle tank 21, *21*
aerial cranes 13, *13*
Airbus A350 27
aircraft
 cargo planes 7, *7*
 engines 26
 fires in 23
 polar planes 25
 see also helicopters
Aircraft Rescue and Firefighting (ARFF) vehicle 23, *23*
ALMA transporter 6, *6*
Antonov An-225 cargo plane 7, *7*
armored vehicles **20–1**
artificial islands 11, *11*
Assault Amphibious Vehicle 21, *21*
Atmospheric Diving Suit (ADS) 36, *36*
augers 16, *16*

Bagger 293 bucket-wheel excavator 8
blast furnaces 28
bomb disposal 32, 33
bridge launchers 20, *20*
bucket chain dredges 10, *10*
bucket-wheel excavators 8, *8*, 9
bulldozers 9, *9*

cargo planes 7, *7*
cars
 armored vehicles 20, 21
 car crushers **30–1**
 engines 27
 metal content 30
 supercars 27
Cassini spacecraft 35, *35*
Caterpillar 797F mining truck 6, *6*
Challenger Deep 37
Channel Tunnel 19, *19*
containerships 27
cranes **12–13**
 aerial cranes 13, *13*
 floating cranes (sheerlegs) 13, *13*
 gantry cranes 12, *12*
 telescopic tower cranes 13, *13*
Curiosity rover 34, *34*
cutter suction dredges 11, *11*

Dante II robot 33, *33*
decompression sickness 36
DeepFlight Challenger submersible 36, *36*
Deepsea Challenger submersible 37, *37*
demolition machines **14–15**
derricks 17, *17*
digging machines *see* excavators
diving suits 36, *36*

dredges **10–11**
 bucket chain dredges 10, *10*
 cutter suction dredges 11, *11*
 grab dredges 11, *11*
drills **16–17**
 augers 16, *16*
 drilling jumbos 17, *17*
 ice core drills 16, *16*
 rotary drills 17, *17*

earth-moving machines **8–9**
emergency vehicles **22–3**
Emma Maersk containership 27, *27*
engines
 diesel engines 27
 jet engines 26
 piston engines 26, 27
Erickson S-64 Aircrane 12, *12*
excavators
 bucket-wheel excavators 8, *8*, 9
 demolition diggers **14–15**, *14–15*
 high-reach excavators 15, *15*
 hydraulic excavators 9
 walking diggers 8, *8*
explosives 15, 16, 19, 32

fire trucks 22, *22*, 23, *23*
floating cranes 13, *13*
flood defenses **38–9**
forging machines 29, *29*

gantry cranes 12, *12*
grab dredges 11, *11*
Grove GTK 1100 tower crane 13

heavy-lift ships 7, *7*
helicopters
 aerial cranes 13, *13*
 rescue helicopters 22, *22*
Hurricane Katrina 39
Huygens space probe 35, *35*
hydraulic excavators 9
hydraulic grippers 30
hydraulic ladders 22, *22*
hydraulic motors 18, *18*
hydraulic presses 31, *31*
hydraulic shears 23, *23*

ice core drills 16, *16*
icebreakers 24, *24*
International Space Station (ISS) 33

"Jaws of Life" 23, *23*
jet engines 26

Koenigsegg Agera R supercar 27, *27*
Komatsu D575 bulldozer 9, *9*

laser cutting machines 28, *28*
lasers 19, 21, 28
lathes 28, *28*

LC-130 Hercules ski plane 25, *25*
loaders 9, *9*
London (Thames Barrier) **38–9**
Lynxs shredder 30

Maeslant barrier 39, *39*
Mariana Trench 37
Mars 34
Mastiff Protected Patrol Vehicle 20, *20*
Menzi Muck A91 excavator 8, *8*
Mercury 34
Messenger spacecraft 34, *34*
metal recovery 30, 31
metalworking **28–9**
mining trucks 6, *6*, 9
MOdulo Sperimentale Elettromeccanico (M.O.S.E.) 39
MV *Blue Marlin* heavy-lift ship 7, *7*

NATO Submarine Rescue Vehicle 23, *23*
Nereus submersible **36–7**, *36–7*
New Horizons spacecraft 35, *35*
New Orleans 39
Newtsuit 36, *36*
nuclear energy 35

oceanic exploration **36–7**
oil rigs 17, *17*
Olympic Games 2012 14

packbots 33, *33*
Palm Jumeirah island 11, *11*
piston engines 26
Pluto 35

rail tunnels **18–19**
railroad snowplows 25, *25*
recyling 30, 31
rescue work 22, 32
road tunnels **18–19**
roadheaders 19, *19*
robots **32–3**, 34
rocket engines 27, *27*
rolling mills 29, *29*
Rolls-Royce Trent XWB engine 26, *26*
rotary drills 17, *17*
Rotterdam 39

Saturn 35, *35*
Saturn V rocket 27, *27*
sheerlegs 13, *13*
ships
 containerships 27
 dredges **10–11**
 floating cranes 13, *13*
 heavy-lift ships 7, *7*
 icebreakers 24, *24*
 semisubmersible ships 7, *7*, 13
 shredders 30, 31, *31*
Sno-Cat 25, *25*
snow blowers 24, *24*
snowplows 25, *25*

Solar and Heliospheric Observatory (SOHO) 34, *34*
solar radiation 34
spacecraft **34–5**
Special Purpose Dexterous Manipulator (Dextre) 33, *33*
steel production 28, 29
submarines 23
submersibles **36–7**
 rescue vehicles 23, *23*
 semisubmersible ships 7, *7*, 13
subzero environments **24–5**, 35
Sun 34

T-52 Enryu robot 32, *32*
Taisun crane 12, *12*
tanks 20, 21
telescopic tower cranes 13, *13*
TEODor robot vehicle 32, *32*
Thames Barrier **38–9**, *38–9*
thermal imagers 20
Titan 35, *35*
Titan Armored Vehicle Launcher Bridge 20, *20*
transporters **6–7**
Triton *36000* submersible 37, *37*
tunnel boring machines (TBMs) **18–19**

Venice 39
volcano exploration 33

Wärtsilä RT-flex96C engine 27, *27*
wrecking balls 15, *15*

Yamal icebreaker 24, *24*